XXXVII. PAPAL ABUSES
XXXVIII. SCENE IN VENICE
XXXIX. PAPAL DOMINION
PART II.
TO THE CLOSE OF THE TROUBLES IN THE REIGN OF CHARLES I
I
II
III. CISTERTIAN MONASTERY
IV
V. MONKS AND SCHOOLMEN
VI. OTHER BENEFITS
VII. CONTINUED
VIII. CRUSADERS
IX
X
XI. TRANSUBSTANTIATION
XII. THE VAUDOIS
XIII
XIV. WALDENSES
XV. ARCHBISHOP CHICHELY TO HENRY V
XVI. WARS OF YORK AND LANCASTER
XVII. WICLIFFE
XVIII. CORRUPTIONS OF THE HIGHER CLERGY
XIX. ABUSE OF MONASTIC POWER
XX. MONASTIC VOLUPTUOUSNESS
XXI. DISSOLUTION OF THE MONASTERIES
XXII. THE SAME SUBJECT
XXIII. CONTINUED
XXIV. SAINTS
XXV. THE VIRGIN
XXVI. APOLOGY
XXVII. IMAGINATIVE REGRETS
XXVIII. REFLECTIONS
XXX. THE POINT AT ISSUE
XXXI. EDWARD VI
XXXII. EDWARD SIGNING THE WARRANT FOR THE EXECUTION OF JOAN OF KENT
XXXIII. REVIVAL OF POPERY
XXXIV. LATIMER AND RIDLEY
XXXV. CRANMER
XXXVI. GENERAL VIEW OF THE TROUBLES OF THE REFORMATION
XXXVII. ENGLISH REFORMERS IN EXILE
XXXVIII. ELIZABETH
XXXIX. EMINENT REFORMERS
XL. THE SAME
XLI. DISTRACTIONS
XLII. GUNPOWDER PLOT
XLIII. THE JUNG-FRAU AND THE FALL OF THE RHINE NEAR SCHAFFHAUSEN
XLIV. TROUBLES OF CHARLES THE FIRST

XLV. LAUD
XLVI. AFFLICTIONS OF ENGLAND
PART III.
FROM THE RESTORATION TO THE PRESENT TIMES
I
II. PATRIOTIC SYMPATHIES
III. CHARLES THE SECOND
IV. LATITUDINARIANISM
V. WALTON'S BOOK OF LIVES
VI. CLERICAL INTEGRITY
VII. PERSECUTION OF THE SCOTTISH COVENANTERS
VIII. ACQUITTAL OF THE BISHOPS
IX. WILLIAM THE THIRD
X. OBLIGATIONS OF CIVIL TO RELIGIOUS LIBERTY
XI. SACHEVEREL
XII
XIII. ASPECTS OF CHRISTIANITY IN AMERICA
I. THE PILGRIM FATHERS
XIV
II. CONTINUED
XV
III. CONCLUDED.--AMERICAN EPISCOPACY
XVI
XVII. PLACES OF WORSHIP
XVIII. PASTORAL CHARACTER
XIX. THE LITURGY
XX. BAPTISM
XXI. SPONSORS
XXII. CATECHISING
XXIII. CONFIRMATION
XXIV. CONFIRMATION CONTINUED
XXV. SACRAMENT
XXVI. THE MARRIAGE CEREMONY
XXVII. THANKSGIVING AFTER CHILDBIRTH
XXVIII. VISITATION OF THE SICK
XXIX. THE COMMINATION SERVICE
XXX. FORMS OF PRAYER AT SEA
XXXI. FUNERAL SERVICE
XXII. RURAL CEREMONY
XXXIII. REGRETS
XXXIV. MUTABILITY
XXXV. OLD ABBEYS
XXXVI. EMIGRANT FRENCH CLERGY
XXXVII. CONGRATULATION
XXXVIII. NEW CHURCHES
XXXIX. CHURCH TO BE ERECTED
XL. CONTINUED
XLI. NEW CHURCHYARD

Ecclesiastical Sonnets by William Wordsworth

IN SERIES, 1821-22.

William Wordsworth was born on 7 April, 1770 in Cockermouth, in Cumbria, northwest England.

Wordsworth spent his early years in his beloved Lake District often with his sister, Dorothy. The English lakes could terrify as well as nurture, and as Wordsworth would write "I grew up fostered alike by beauty and by fear,"

After being schooled at Hawkshead he went to St. John's College, Cambridge but not liking the competitive nature of the place idled his way through saying he "was not for that hour, nor for that place."

Whilst still at Cambridge he travelled to France. He was immediately taken by the Revolutionary fervor and the confluence of a set of great ideals and rallying calls for the people of France.

In his early twenties he ventured again to France and fathered an illegitimate child. He would not see that daughter till she was 9 owing to the tensions and hostilities between England and France.

There now followed a period of three to four years that plagued Wordsworth with doubt. He was now in his early thirties but had no profession, was rootless and virtually penniless.

Although his career was not on track he did manage to publish two volumes, both in 1793; An Evening Walk and Descriptive Sketches.

This dark period ended in 1795. A legacy of £900 received from Raisley Calvert enabled Wordsworth to pursue a literary career in earnest.

In 1797 he became great friends with a fellow poet, Samuel Taylor Coleridge. They formed a partnership that would change both their lives and the course of English poetry.

Their aim was for a decisive break with the strictures of Neoclassical verse. In 1798 the ground breaking Lyrical Ballads was published. Wordsworth wrote in the preface "the spontaneous overflow of powerful feelings: it takes its origin from emotion recollected in tranquility." Most of the poems were dramatic in form, designed to reveal the character of the speaker. Thus the poems set forth a new style, a new vocabulary, and new subjects for poetry.

Coleridge had also conceived of an enormous poem to be called "The Brook," in which he proposed to treat all science, philosophy, and religion, but soon laid the burden of writing it to Wordsworth. To test his powers for that endeavour, Wordsworth began writing the autobiographical poem that would absorb him for the next 40 years, and which was eventually published as The Prelude, or, Growth of a Poet's Mind.

By the 1820s, the critical acclaim for Wordsworth was growing, but perhaps his best years of work were behind him. Nonetheless he continued to write and to revise previous works.

With the death is 1843 of his friend and Poet Laureate Robert Southey, Wordsworth was offered the position. He accepted despite saying he wouldn't write any poetry as Poet Laureate. And indeed he didn't.

Wordsworth died of pleurisy on 23 April 1850. He was buried in St Oswald's church Grasmere.

Index of Contents
PART I.
FROM THE INTRODUCTION OF CHRISTIANITY INTO BRITAIN, TO THE CONSUMMATION OF THE PAPAL DOMINION
I. INTRODUCTION
II. CONJECTURES
III. TREPIDATION OF THE DRUIDS
IV. DRUIDICAL EXCOMMUNICATION
V. UNCERTAINTY
VI. PERSECUTION
VII. RECOVERY
VIII. TEMPTATIONS FROM ROMAN REFINEMENTS
IX. DISSENSIONS
X. STRUGGLE OF THE BRITONS AGAINST THE BARBARIANS
XI. SAXON CONQUEST
XII. MONASTERY OF OLD BANGOR
XIII. CASUAL INCITEMENT
XIV. GLAD TIDINGS
XV. PAULINUS
XVI. PERSUASION
XVII. CONVERSION
XVIII. APOLOGY
XIX. PRIMITIVE SAXON CLERGY
XX. OTHER INFLUENCES
XXI. SECLUSION
XXII. CONTINUED
XXIII. REPROOF
XXIV. SAXON MONASTERIES, AND LIGHTS AND SHADES OF THE RELIGION
XXV. MISSIONS AND TRAVELS
XXVI. ALFRED
XXVII. HIS DESCENDANTS
XXVIII. INFLUENCE ABUSED
XXIX. DANISH CONQUESTS
XXX. CANUTE
XXXI. THE NORMAN CONQUEST
XXXII
XXXIII. THE COUNCIL OF CLERMONT
XXXIV. CRUSADES
XXXV. RICHARD I
XXXVI. AN INTERDICT

XLII. CATHEDRALS, ETC.
XLIII. INSIDE OF KING'S COLLEGE CHAPEL, CAMBRIDGE
XLIV. THE SAME
XLV. CONTINUED
XLVI. EJACULATION
XLVII. CONCLUSION
WILLIAM WORDSWORTH – A SHORT BIOGRAPHY
WILLIAM WORDSWORTH – A CONCISE BIBLIOGRAPHY

PART I.

FROM THE INTRODUCTION OF CHRISTIANITY INTO BRITAIN, TO THE CONSUMMATION OF THE PAPAL DOMINION

"A verse may catch a wandering Soul, that flies
Profounder Tracts, and by a blest surprise
Convert delight into a Sacrifice."

I. INTRODUCTION

I, who accompanied with faithful pace
Cerulean Duddon from his cloud-fed spring,
And loved with spirit ruled by his to sing
Of mountain quiet and boon nature's grace;
I, who essayed the nobler Stream to trace
Of Liberty, and smote the plausive string
Till the checked torrent, proudly triumphing,
Won for herself a lasting resting-place;
Now seek upon the heights of Time the source
Of a HOLY RIVER, on whose banks are found
Sweet pastoral flowers, and laurels that have crowned
Full oft the unworthy brow of lawless force;
And, for delight of him who tracks its course,
Immortal amaranth and palms abound.

II. CONJECTURES

If there be prophets on whose spirits rest
Past things, revealed like future, they can tell
What Powers, presiding o'er the sacred well
Of Christian Faith, this savage Island blessed
With its first bounty. Wandering through the west,
Did holy Paul a while in Britain dwell,

And call the Fountain forth by miracle,
And with dread signs the nascent Stream invest?
Or He, whose bonds dropped off, whose prison doors
Flew open, by an Angel's voice unbarred?
Or some of humbler name, to these wild shores
Storm-driven; who, having seen the cup of woe
Pass from their Master, sojourned here to guard
The precious Current they had taught to flow?

III. TREPIDATION OF THE DRUIDS

Screams round the Arch-druid's brow the seamew--white
As Menai's foam; and toward the mystic ring
Where Augurs stand, the Future questioning,
Slowly the cormorant aims her heavy flight,
Portending ruin to each baleful rite,
That, in the lapse of ages, hath crept o'er
Diluvian truths, and patriarchal lore.
Haughty the Bard: can these meek doctrines blight
His transports? wither his heroic strains?
But all shall be fulfilled;--the Julian spear
A way first opened; and, with Roman chains,
The tidings come of Jesus crucified;
They come--they spread--the weak, the suffering, hear;
Receive the faith, and in the hope abide.

IV. DRUIDICAL EXCOMMUNICATION

Mercy and Love have met thee on thy road,
Thou wretched Outcast, from the gift of fire
And food cut off by sacerdotal ire,
From every sympathy that Man bestowed!
Yet shall it claim our reverence, that to God,
Ancient of days! that to the eternal Sire,
These jealous Ministers of law aspire,
As to the one sole fount whence wisdom flowed,
Justice, and order. Tremblingly escaped,
As if with prescience of the coming storm,
'That' intimation when the stars were shaped;
And still, 'mid yon thick woods, the primal truth
Glimmers through many a superstitious form
That fills the Soul with unavailing ruth.

V. UNCERTAINTY

Darkness surrounds us; seeking, we are lost
On Snowdon's wilds, amid Brigantian coves,
Or where the solitary shepherd roves
Along the plain of Sarum, by the ghost
Of Time and shadows of Tradition, crost;
And where the boatman of the Western Isles
Slackens his course--to mark those holy piles
Which yet survive on bleak Iona's coast.
Nor these, nor monuments of eldest name,
Nor Taliesin's unforgotten lays,
Nor characters of Greek or Roman fame,
To an unquestionable Source have led;
Enough--if eyes, that sought the fountainhead
In vain, upon the growing Rill may gaze.

VI. PERSECUTION

Lament! for Diocletian's fiery sword
Works busy as the lightning; but instinct
With malice ne'er to deadliest weapon linked
Which God's ethereal store-houses afford:
Against the Followers of the incarnate Lord
It rages; some are smitten in the field--
Some pierced to the heart through the ineffectual shield
Of sacred home;--with pomp are others gored
And dreadful respite. Thus was Alban tried,
England's first Martyr, whom no threats could shake;
Self-offered victim, for his friend he died,
And for the faith; nor shall his name forsake
That Hill, whose flowery platform seems to rise
By Nature decked for holiest sacrifice.

VII. RECOVERY

As, when a storm hath ceased, the birds regain
Their cheerfulness, and busily retrim
Their nests, or chant a gratulating hymn
To the blue ether and bespangled plain;
Even so, in many a re-constructed fane,
Have the survivors of this Storm renewed
Their holy rites with vocal gratitude:

And solemn ceremonials they ordain
To celebrate their great deliverance;
Most feelingly instructed 'mid their fear--
That persecution, blind with rage extreme,
May not the less, through Heaven's mild countenance,
Even in her own despite, both feed and cheer;
For all things are less dreadful than they seem.

VIII. TEMPTATIONS FROM ROMAN REFINEMENTS

Watch, and be firm! for, soul-subduing vice,
Heart-killing luxury, on your steps await.
Fair houses, baths, and banquets delicate,
And temples flashing, bright as polar ice,
Their radiance through the woods--may yet suffice
To sap your hardy virtue, and abate
Your love of Him upon whose forehead sate
The crown of thorns; whose life-blood flowed, the price
Of your redemption. Shun the insidious arts
That Rome provides, less dreading from her frown
Than from her wily praise, her peaceful gown,
Language, and letters;--these, though fondly viewed
As humanising graces, are but parts
And instruments of deadliest servitude!

IX. DISSENSIONS

That heresies should strike (if truth be scanned
Presumptuously) their roots both wide and deep,
Is natural as dreams to feverish sleep.
Lo! Discord at the altar dares to stand
Uplifting toward high Heaven her fiery brand,
A cherished Priestess of the new-baptized!
But chastisement shall follow peace despised.
The Pictish cloud darkens the enervate land
By Rome abandoned; vain are suppliant cries,
And prayers that would undo her forced farewell;
For she returns not.--Awed by her own knell,
She casts the Britons upon strange Allies
Soon to become more dreaded enemies
Than heartless misery called them to repel.

X. STRUGGLE OF THE BRITONS AGAINST THE BARBARIANS

Rise!--they 'have' risen: of brave Aneurin ask
How they have scourged old foes, perfidious friends:
The Spirit of Caractacus descends
Upon the Patriots, animates their task;--
Amazement runs before the towering casque
Of Arthur, bearing through the stormy field
The virgin sculptured on his Christian shield:--
Stretched in the sunny light of victory bask
The Host that followed Urien as he strode
O'er heaps of slain;--from Cambrian wood and moss
Druids descend, auxiliars of the Cross;
Bards, nursed on blue Plinlimmon's still abode,
Rush on the fight, to harps preferring swords,
And everlasting deeds to burning words!

XI. SAXON CONQUEST

Nor wants the cause the panic-striking aid
Of hallelujahs tost from hill to hill--
For instant victory. But Heaven's high will
Permits a second and a darker shade
Of Pagan night. Afflicted and dismayed,
The Relics of the sword flee to the mountains:
O wretched Land! whose tears have flowed like fountains;
Whose arts and honours in the dust are laid
By men yet scarcely conscious of a care
For other monuments than those of Earth;
Who, as the fields and woods have given them birth,
Will build their savage fortunes only there;
Content, if foss, and barrow, and the girth
Of long-drawn rampart, witness what they were.

XII. MONASTERY OF OLD BANGOR

'The oppression of the tumult--wrath and scorn--
The tribulation--and the gleaming blades'--
Such is the impetuous spirit that pervades
The song of Taliesin;--Ours shall mourn
The 'unarmed' Host who by their prayers would turn
The sword from Bangor's walls, and guard the store
Of Aboriginal and Roman lore,
And Christian monuments, that now must burn

To senseless ashes. Mark! how all things swerve
From their known course, or vanish like a dream;
Another language spreads from coast to coast;
Only perchance some melancholy Stream
And some indignant Hills old names preserve,
When laws, and creeds, and people all are lost!

XIII. CASUAL INCITEMENT

A bright-haired company of youthful slaves,
Beautiful strangers, stand within the pale
Of a sad market, ranged for public sale,
Where Tiber's stream the immortal City laves:
ANGLI by name; and not an ANGEL waves
His wing who could seem lovelier to man's eye
Than they appear to holy Gregory;
Who, having learnt that name, salvation craves
For Them, and for their Land. The earnest Sire,
His questions urging, feels, in slender ties
Of chiming sound, commanding sympathies;
DE-IRIANS--he would save them from God's IRE;
Subjects of Saxon AELLA--they shall sing
Glad HALLE-lujahs to the eternal King!

XIV. GLAD TIDINGS

For ever hallowed be this morning fair,
Blest be the unconscious shore on which ye tread,
And blest the silver Cross, which ye, instead
Of martial banner, in procession bear;
The Cross preceding Him who floats in air,
The pictured Saviour!--By Augustin led,
They come--and onward travel without dread,
Chanting in barbarous ears a tuneful prayer--
Sung for themselves, and those whom they would free!
Rich conquest waits them:--the tempestuous sea
Of Ignorance, that ran so rough and high
And heeded not the voice of clashing swords,
These good men humble by a few bare words,
And calm with fear of God's divinity.

XV. PAULINUS

But, to remote Northumbria's royal Hall,
Where thoughtful Edwin, tutored in the school
Of sorrow, still maintains a heathen rule,
'Who' comes with functions apostolical?
Mark him, of shoulders curved, and stature tall,
Black hair, and vivid eye, and meagre cheek,
His prominent feature like an eagle's beak;
A Man whose aspect doth at once appal
And strike with reverence. The Monarch leans
Toward the pure truths this Delegate propounds
Repeatedly his own deep mind he sounds
With careful hesitation,--then convenes
A synod of his Councillors:--give ear,
And what a pensive Sage doth utter, hear!

XVI. PERSUASION

"Man's life is like a Sparrow, mighty King!
"That--while at banquet with your Chiefs you sit
"Housed near a blazing fire--is seen to flit
"Safe from the wintry tempest. Fluttering,
"Here did it enter; there, on hasty wing,
"Flies out, and passes on from cold to cold;
"But whence it came we know not, nor behold
"Whither it goes. Even such, that transient Thing,
"The human Soul; not utterly unknown
"While in the Body lodged, her warm abode;
"But from what world She came, what woe or weal
"On her departure waits, no tongue hath shown;
"This mystery if the Stranger can reveal,
"His be a welcome cordially bestowed!"

XVII. CONVERSION

Prompt transformation works the novel Lore;
The Council closed, the Priest in full career
Rides forth, an armed man, and hurls a spear
To desecrate the Fane which heretofore
He served in folly. Woden falls, and Thor
Is overturned; the mace, in battle heaved
(So might they dream) till victory was achieved,
Drops, and the God himself is seen no more.
Temple and Altar sink, to hide their shame

Amid oblivious weeds. "O come to me,
Ye heavy laden!" such the inviting voice
Heard near fresh streams; and thousands who rejoice
In the new Rite, the pledge of sanctity,
Shall, by regenerate life, the promise claim.

XVIII. APOLOGY

Nor scorn the aid which Fancy oft doth lend
The Soul's eternal interests to promote:
Death, darkness, danger, are our natural lot;
And evil Spirits 'may' our walk attend
For aught the wisest know or comprehend;
Then be 'good' Spirits free to breathe a note
Of elevation; let their odours float
Around these Converts; and their glories blend,
The midnight stars outshining, or the blaze
Of the noon-day. Nor doubt that golden cords
Of good works, mingling with the visions, raise
The Soul to purer worlds: and 'who' the line
Shall draw, the limits of the power define,
That even imperfect faith to man affords?

XIX. PRIMITIVE SAXON CLERGY

How beautiful your presence, how benign,
Servants of God! who not a thought will share
With the vain world; who, outwardly as bare
As winter trees, yield no fallacious sign
That the firm soul is clothed with fruit divine!
Such Priest, when service worthy of his care
Has called him forth to breathe the common air,
Might seem a saintly Image from its shrine
Descended:--happy are the eyes that meet
The Apparition; evil thoughts are stayed
At his approach, and low-bowed necks entreat
A benediction from his voice or hand;
Whence grace, through which the heart can understand,
And vows, that bind the will, in silence made.

XX. OTHER INFLUENCES

Ah, when the Body, round which in love we clung,
Is chilled by death, does mutual service fail?
Is tender pity then of no avail?
Are intercessions of the fervent tongue
A waste of hope?--From this sad source have sprung
Rites that console the Spirit, under grief
Which ill can brook more rational relief:
Hence, prayers are shaped amiss, and dirges sung
For Souls whose doom is fixed! The way is smooth
For Power that travels with the human heart:
Confession ministers the pang to soothe
In him who at the ghost of guilt doth start.
Ye holy Men, so earnest in your care,
Of your own mighty instruments beware!

XXI. SECLUSION

Lance, shield, and sword relinquished, at his side
A bead-roll, in his hand a clasped book,
Or staff more harmless than a shepherd's crook,
The war-worn Chieftain quits the world--to hide
His thin autumnal locks where Monks abide
In cloistered privacy. But not to dwell
In soft repose he comes: within his cell,
Round the decaying trunk of human pride,
At morn, and eve, and midnight's silent hour,
Do penitential cogitations cling;
Like ivy, round some ancient elm, they twine
In grisly folds and strictures serpentine;
Yet, while they strangle, a fair growth they bring,
For recompence--their own perennial bower.

XXII. CONTINUED

Methinks that to some vacant hermitage
'My' feet would rather turn--to some dry nook
Scooped out of living rock, and near a brook
Hurled down a mountain-cove from stage to stage,
Yet tempering, for my sight, its bustling rage
In the soft heaven of a translucent pool;
Thence creeping under sylvan arches cool,
Fit haunt of shapes whose glorious equipage
Would elevate my dreams. A beechen bowl,
A maple dish, my furniture should be;

Crisp, yellow leaves my bed; the hooting owl
My night-watch: nor should e'er the crested fowl
From thorp or vill his matins sound for me,
Tired of the world and all its industry.

XXIII. REPROOF

But what if One, through grove or flowery mead,
Indulging thus at will the creeping feet
Of a voluptuous indolence, should meet
Thy hovering Shade, O venerable Bede!
The saint, the scholar, from a circle freed
Of toil stupendous, in a hallowed seat
Of learning, where thou heard'st the billows beat
On a wild coast, rough monitors to feed
Perpetual industry. Sublime Recluse!
The recreant soul, that dares to shun the debt
Imposed on human kind, must first forget
Thy diligence, thy unrelaxing use
Of a long life; and, in the hour of death,
The last dear service of thy passing breath!

XXIV. SAXON MONASTERIES, AND LIGHTS AND SHADES OF THE RELIGION

By such examples moved to unbought pains,
The people work like congregated bees;
Eager to build the quiet Fortresses
Where Piety, as they believe, obtains
From Heaven a 'general' blessing; timely rains
Or needful sunshine; prosperous enterprise,
Justice and peace:--bold faith! yet also rise
The sacred Structures for less doubtful gains.
The Sensual think with reverence of the palms
Which the chaste Votaries seek, beyond the grave
If penance be redeemable, thence alms
Flow to the poor, and freedom to the slave;
And if full oft the Sanctuary save
Lives black with guilt, ferocity it calms.

XXV. MISSIONS AND TRAVELS

Not sedentary all: there are who roam

To scatter seeds of life on barbarous shores;
Or quit with zealous step their knee-worn floors
To seek the general mart of Christendom;
Whence they, like richly-laden merchants, come
To their beloved cells:--or shall we say
That, like the Red-cross Knight, they urge their way,
To lead in memorable triumph home
Truth, their immortal Una? Babylon,
Learned and wise, hath perished utterly,
Nor leaves her Speech one word to aid the sigh
That would lament her;--Memphis, Tyre, are gone
With all their Arts,--but classic lore glides on
By these Religious saved for all posterity.

XXVI. ALFRED

Behold a pupil of the monkish gown,
The pious ALFRED, King to Justice dear!
Lord of the harp and liberating spear;
Mirror of Princes! Indigent Renown
Might range the starry ether for a crown
Equal to 'his' deserts, who, like the year,
Pours forth his bounty, like the day doth cheer,
And awes like night with mercy-tempered frown.
Ease from this noble miser of his time
No moment steals; pain narrows not his cares.
Though small his kingdom as a spark or gem,
Of Alfred boasts remote Jerusalem,
And Christian India, through her widespread clime,
In sacred converse gifts with Alfred shares.

XXVII. HIS DESCENDANTS

When thy great soul was freed from mortal chains,
Darling of England! many a bitter shower
Fell on thy tomb; but emulative power
Flowed in thy line through undegenerate veins.
The Race of Alfred covet glorious pains
When dangers threaten, dangers ever new!
Black tempests bursting, blacker still in view!
But manly sovereignty its hold retains;
The root sincere, the branches bold to strive
With the fierce tempest, while, within the round
Of their protection, gentle virtues thrive;

As oft, 'mid some green plot of open ground,
Wide as the oak extends its dewy gloom,
The fostered hyacinths spread their purple bloom.

XXVIII. INFLUENCE ABUSED

Urged by Ambition, who with subtlest skill
Changes her means, the Enthusiast as a dupe
Shall soar, and as a hypocrite can stoop,
And turn the instruments of good to ill,
Moulding the credulous people to his will.
Such DUNSTAN:--from its Benedictine coop
Issues the master Mind, at whose fell swoop
The chaste affections tremble to fulfil
Their purposes. Behold, pre-signified,
The Might of spiritual sway! his thoughts, his dreams,
Do in the supernatural world abide:
So vaunt a throng of Followers, filled with pride
In what they see of virtues pushed to extremes,
And sorceries of talent misapplied.

XXIX. DANISH CONQUESTS

Woe to the Crown that doth the Cowl obey!
Dissension, checking arms that would restrain
The incessant Rovers of the northern main,
Helps to restore and spread a Pagan sway:
But Gospel-truth is potent to allay
Fierceness and rage; and soon the cruel Dane
Feels, through the influence of her gentle reign,
His native superstitions melt away.
Thus, often, when thick gloom the east o'ershrouds,
The full-orbed Moon, slow-climbing, doth appear
Silently to consume the heavy clouds;
'How' no one can resolve; but every eye
Around her sees, while air is hushed, a clear
And widening circuit of ethereal sky.

XXX. CANUTE

A pleasant music floats along the Mere,
From Monks in Ely chanting service high,

While-as Canute the King is rowing by:
"My Oarsmen," quoth the mighty King, "draw near,
"That we the sweet song of the Monks may hear!"
He listens (all past conquests, and all schemes
Of future, vanishing like empty dreams)
Heart-touched, and haply not without a tear.
The Royal Minstrel, ere the choir is still,
While his free Barge skims the smooth flood along,
Gives to that rapture an accordant Rhyme.
O suffering Earth! be thankful: sternest clime
And rudest age are subject to the thrill
Of heaven-descended Piety and Song.

XXXI. THE NORMAN CONQUEST

The woman-hearted Confessor prepares
The evanescence of the Saxon line.
Hark! 'tis the tolling Curfew!--the stars shine;
But of the lights that cherish houschold cares
And festive gladness, burns not one that dares
To twinkle after that dull stroke of thine,
Emblem and instrument, from Thames to Tyne,
Of force that daunts, and cunning that ensnares!
Yet as the terrors of the lordly bell,
That quench, from hut to palace, lamps and fires,
Touch not the tapers of the sacred quires;
Even so a thraldom, studious to expel
Old laws, and ancient customs to derange,
To Creed or Ritual brings no fatal change.

XXXII

Coldy we spake. The Saxons, overpowered
By wrong triumphant through its own excess,
From fields laid waste, from house and home devoured
By flames, look up to heaven and crave redress
From God's eternal justice. Pitiless
Though men be, there are angels that can feel
For wounds that death alone has power to heal,
For penitent guilt, and innocent distress.
And has a Champion risen in arms to try
His Country's virtue, fought, and breathes no more;
Him in their hearts the people canonize;
And far above the mine's most precious ore

The least small pittance of bare mould they prize
Scooped from the sacred earth where his dear relics lie.

XXXIII. THE COUNCIL OF CLERMONT

"And shall," the Pontiff asks, "profaneness flow
"From Nazareth--source of Christian piety,
"From Bethlehem, from the Mounts of Agony
"And glorified Ascension? Warriors, go,
"With prayers and blessings we your path will sow;
"Like Moses hold our hands erect, till ye
"Have chased far off by righteous victory
"These sons of Amalek, or laid them low!"--
"GOD WILLETH IT," the whole assembly cry;
Shout which the enraptured multitude astounds!
The Council-roof and Clermont's towers reply;--
"God willeth it," from hill to hill rebounds,
And, in awe-stricken Countries far and nigh,
Through "Nature's hollow arch" that voice resounds.

XXXIV. CRUSADES

The turbaned Race are poured in thickening swarms
Along the west; though driven from Aquitaine,
The Crescent glitters on the towers of Spain;
And soft Italia feels renewed alarms;
The scimitar, that yields not to the charms
Of ease, the narrow Bosphorus will disdain;
Nor long (that crossed) would Grecian hills detain
Their tents, and check the current of their arms.
Then blame not those who, by the mightiest lever
Known to the moral world, Imagination,
Upheave, so seems it, from her natural station
All Christendom:--they sweep along (was never
So huge a host!)--to tear from the Unbeliever
The precious Tomb, their haven of salvation.

XXXV. RICHARD I

Redoubted King, of courage leonine,
I mark thee, Richard! urgent to equip
Thy warlike person with the staff and scrip;

I watch thee sailing o'er the midland brine;
In conquered Cyprus see thy Bride decline
Her blushing cheek, love-vows upon her lip,
And see love-emblems streaming from thy ship,
As thence she holds her way to Palestine.
My Song, a fearless homager, would attend
Thy thundering battle-axe as it cleaves the press
Of war, but duty summons her away
To tell--how, finding in the rash distress
Of those Enthusiasts a subservient friend,
To giddier heights hath clomb the Papal sway.

XXXVI. AN INTERDICT

Realms quake by turns: proud Arbitress of grace,
The Church, by mandate shadowing forth the power
She arrogates o'er heaven's eternal door,
Closes the gates of every sacred place.
Straight from the sun and tainted air's embrace
All sacred things are covered: cheerful morn
Grows sad as night--no seemly garb is worn,
Nor is a face allowed to meet a face
With natural smiles of greeting. Bells are dumb;
Ditches are graves--funereal rites denied;
And in the churchyard he must take his bride
Who dares be wedded! Fancies thickly come
Into the pensive heart ill fortified,
And comfortless despairs the soul benumb.

XXXVII. PAPAL ABUSES

As with the Stream our voyage we pursue,
The gross materials of this world present
A marvellous study of wild accident;
Uncouth proximities of old and new;
And bold transfigurations, more untrue
(As might be deemed) to disciplined intent
Than aught the sky's fantastic element,
When most fantastic, offers to the view.
Saw we not Henry scourged at Becket's shrine?
Lo! John self-stripped of his insignia:--crown,
Sceptre and mantle, sword and ring, laid down
At a proud Legate's feet! The spears that line
Baronial halls, the opprobrious insult feel;

And angry Ocean roars a vain appeal.

XXXVIII. SCENE IN VENICE

Black Demons hovering o'er his mitred head,
To Caesar's Successor the Pontiff spake;
"Ere I absolve thee, stoop! that on thy neck
"Levelled with earth this foot of mine may tread."
Then he, who to the altar had been led,
He, whose strong arm the Orient could not check,
He, who had held the Soldan at his beck,
Stooped, of all glory disinherited,
And even the common dignity of man!--
Amazement strikes the crowd: while many turn
Their eyes away in sorrow, others burn
With scorn, invoking a vindictive ban
From outraged Nature; but the sense of most
In abject sympathy with power is lost.

XXXIX. PAPAL DOMINION

Unless to Peter's Chair the viewless wind
Must come and ask permission when to blow,
What further empire would it have? for now
A ghostly Domination, unconfined
As that by dreaming Bards to Love assigned,
Sits there in sober truth--to raise the low,
Perplex the wise, the strong to overthrow;
Through earth and heaven to bind and to unbind!--
Resist--the thunder quails thee!--crouch--rebuff
Shall be thy recompence! from land to land
The ancient thrones of Christendom are stuff
For occupation of a magic wand,
And 'tis the Pope that wields it:--whether rough
Or smooth his front, our world is in his hand!

PART II.

TO THE CLOSE OF THE TROUBLES IN THE REIGN OF CHARLES I

I

How soon--alas! did Man, created pure--
By Angels guarded, deviate from the line
Prescribed to duty:--woeful forfeiture
He made by wilful breach of law divine.
With like perverseness did the Church abjure
Obedience to her Lord, and haste to twine,
'Mid Heaven-born flowers that shall for aye endure,
Weeds on whose front the world had fixed her sign.
O Man,--if with thy trials thus it fares,
If good can smooth the way to evil choice,
From all rash censure be the mind kept free;
He only judges right who weighs, compares,
And in the sternest sentence which his voice
Pronounces, ne'er abandons Charity.

II

From false assumption rose, and, fondly hailed
By superstition, spread the Papal power;
Yet do not deem the Autocracy prevailed
Thus only, even in error's darkest hour.
She daunts, forth-thundering from her spiritual tower,
Brute rapine, or with gentle lure she tames.
Justice and Peace through Her uphold their claims;
And Chastity finds many a sheltering bower.
Realm there is none that if controlled or swayed
By her commands partakes not, in degree,
Of good, o'er manners arts and arms, diffused:
Yes, to thy domination, Roman See,
Tho' miserably, oft monstrously, abused
By blind ambition, be this tribute paid.

III. CISTERTIAN MONASTERY

"Here Man more purely lives, less oft doth fall,
"More promptly rises, walks with stricter heed,
"More safely rests, dies happier, is freed
"Earlier from cleansing fires, and gains withal
"A brighter crown."--On yon Cistertian wall
'That' confident assurance may be read;
And, to like shelter, from the world have fled
Increasing multitudes. The potent call
Doubtless shall cheat full oft the heart's desires;

Yet, while the rugged Age on pliant knee
Vows to rapt Fancy humble fealty,
A gentler life spreads round the holy spires;
Where'er they rise, the sylvan waste retires,
And aery harvests crown the fertile lea.

IV

Deplorable his lot who tills the ground,
His whole life long tills it, with heartless toil
Of villain-service, passing with the soil
To each new Master, like a steer or hound,
Or like a rooted tree, or stone earth-bound;
But mark how gladly, through their own domains,
The Monks relax or break these iron chains;
While Mercy, uttering, through their voice, a sound
Echoed in Heaven, cries out, "Ye Chiefs, abate
These legalized oppressions! Man--whose name
And nature God disdained not; Man--whose soul
Christ died for--cannot forfeit his high claim
To live and move exempt from all control
Which fellow-feeling doth not mitigate!"

V. MONKS AND SCHOOLMEN

Record we too, with just and faithful pen,
That many hooded Cenobites there are,
Who in their private cells have yet a care
Of public quiet; unambitious Men,
Counsellors for the world, of piercing ken;
Whose fervent exhortations from afar
Move Princes to their duty, peace or war;
And oft-times in the most forbidding den
Of solitude, with love of science strong,
How patiently the yoke of thought they bear
How subtly glide its finest threads along!
Spirits that crowd the intellectual sphere
With mazy boundaries, as the astronomer
With orb and cycle girds the starry throng.

VI. OTHER BENEFITS

And, not in vain embodied to the sight,
Religion finds even in the stern retreat
Of feudal sway her own appropriate seat;
From the collegiate pomps on Windsor's height
Down to the humbler altar, which the Knight
And his retainers of the embattled hall
Seek in domestic oratory small,
For prayer in stillness, or the chanted rite;
Then chiefly dear, when foes are planted round,
Who teach the intrepid guardians of the place--
Hourly exposed to death, with famine worn,
And suffering under many a perilous wound--
How sad would be their durance, if forlorn
Of offices dispensing heavenly grace!

VII. CONTINUED

And what melodious sounds at times prevail!
And, ever and anon, how bright a gleam
Pours on the surface of the turbid Stream!
What heartfelt fragrance mingles with the gale
That swells the bosom of our passing sail!
For where, but on 'this' River's margin, blow
Those flowers of chivalry, to bind the brow
Of hardihood with wreaths that shall not fail?--
Fair Court of Edward! wonder of the world!
I see a matchless blazonry unfurled
Of wisdom, magnanimity, and love;
And meekness tempering honourable pride;
The lamb is couching by the lion's side,
And near the flame-eyed eagle sits the dove.

VIII. CRUSADERS

Furl we the sails, and pass with tardy oars
Through these bright regions, casting many a glance
Upon the dream-like issues--the romance
Of many-coloured life that Fortune pours
Round the Crusaders, till on distant shores
Their labours end; or they return to lie,
The vow performed, in cross-legged effigy,
Devoutly stretched upon their chancel floors.
Am I deceived? Or is their requiem chanted
By voices never mute when Heaven unties

Her inmost, softest, tenderest harmonies;
Requiem which Earth takes up with voice undaunted,
When she would tell how Brave, and Good, and Wise,
For their high guerdon not in vain have panted!

IX

As faith thus sanctified the warrior's crest
While from the Papal Unity there came,
What feebler means had failed to give, one aim
Diffused thro' all the regions of the West;
So does her Unity its power attest
By works of Art, that shed, on the outward frame
Of worship, glory and grace, which who shall blame
That ever looked to heaven for final rest?
Hail countless Temples! that so well befit
Your ministry; that, as ye rise and take
Form spirit and character from holy writ,
Give to devotion, wheresoe'er awake,
Pinions of high and higher sweep, and make
The unconverted soul with awe submit.

X

Where long and deeply hath been fixed the root
In the blest soil of gospel truth, the Tree,
(Blighted or scathed tho' many branches be,
Put forth to wither, many a hopeful shoot)
Can never cease to bear celestial fruit.
Witness the Church that oft-times, with effect
Dear to the saints, strives earnestly to eject
Her bane, her vital energies recruit.
Lamenting, do not hopelessly repine,
When such good work is doomed to be undone,
The conquests lost that were so hardly won:--
All promises vouchsafed by Heaven will shine
In light confirmed while years their course shall run,
Confirmed alike in progress and decline.

XI. TRANSUBSTANTIATION

Enough! for see, with dim association

The tapers burn; the odorous incense feeds
A greedy flame; the pompous mass proceeds;
The Priest bestows the appointed consecration;
And, while the HOST is raised, its elevation
An awe and supernatural horror breeds;
And all the people bow their heads, like reeds
To a soft breeze, in lowly adoration.
This Valdo brooks not. On the banks of Rhone
He taught, till persecution chased him thence,
To adore the Invisible, and Him alone.
Nor are his Followers loth to seek defence,
'Mid woods and wilds, on Nature's craggy throne,
From rites that trample upon soul and sense.

XII. THE VAUDOIS

But whence came they who for the Saviour Lord
Have long borne witness as the Scriptures teach?--
Ages ere Valdo raised his voice to preach
In Gallic ears the unadulterate Word,
Their fugitive Progenitors explored
Subalpine vales, in quest of safe retreats
Where that pure Church survives, though summer heats
Open a passage to the Romish sword,
Far as it dares to follow. Herbs self-sown,
And fruitage gathered from the chestnut wood,
Nourish the sufferers then; and mists, that brood
O'er chasms with new-fallen obstacles bestrown,
Protect them; and the eternal snow that daunts
Aliens, is God's good winter for their haunts.

XIII

Praised be the Rivers, from their mountain springs
Shouting to Freedom, "Plant thy banners here!"
To harassed Piety, "Dismiss thy fear,
And in our caverns smooth thy ruffled wings!"
Nor be unthanked their final lingerings--
Silent, but not to high-souled Passion's ear--
'Mid reedy fens wide-spread and marshes drear,
Their own creation. Such glad welcomings
As Po was heard to give where Venice rose
Hailed from aloft those Heirs of truth divine
Who near his fountains sought obscure repose,

Yet came prepared as glorious lights to shine,
Should that be needed for their sacred Charge;
Blest Prisoners They, whose spirits were at large!

XIV. WALDENSES

Those had given earliest notice, as the lark
Springs from the ground the morn to gratulate;
Or rather rose the day to antedate,
By striking out a solitary spark,
When all the world with midnight gloom was dark.--
Then followed the Waldensian bands, whom Hate
In vain endeavours to exterminate,
Whom Obloquy pursues with hideous bark:
But they desist not;--and the sacred fire,
Rekindled thus, from dens and savage woods
Moves, handed on with never-ceasing care,
Through courts, through camps, o'er limitary floods;
Nor lacks this sea-girt Isle a timely share
Of the new Flame, not suffered to expire.

XV. ARCHBISHOP CHICHELY TO HENRY V

"What beast in wilderness or cultured field
"The lively beauty of the leopard shows?
"What flower in meadow-ground or garden grows
"That to the towering lily doth not yield?
"Let both meet only on thy royal shield!
"Go forth, great King! claim what thy birth bestows;
"Conquer the Gallic lily which thy foes
"Dare to usurp;--thou hast a sword to wield,
"And Heaven will crown the right."--The mitred Sire
Thus spake--and lo! a Fleet, for Gaul addrest,
Ploughs her bold course across the wondering seas;
For, sooth to say, ambition, in the breast
Of youthful heroes, is no sullen fire,
But one that leaps to meet the fanning breeze.

XVI. WARS OF YORK AND LANCASTER

Thus is the storm abated by the craft
Of a shrewd Counsellor, eager to protect

The Church, whose power hath recently been checked,
Whose monstrous riches threatened. So the shaft
Of victory mounts high, and blood is quaffed
In fields that rival Cressy and Poictiers--
Pride to be washed away by bitter tears!
For deep as Hell itself, the avenging draught
Of civil slaughter. Yet, while temporal power
Is by these shocks exhausted, spiritual truth
Maintains the else endangered gift of life;
Proceeds from infancy to lusty youth;
And, under cover of this woeful strife,
Gathers unblighted strength from hour to hour.

XVII. WICLIFFE

Once more the Church is seized with sudden fear,
And at her call is Wicliffe disinhumed:
Yea, his dry bones to ashes are consumed
And flung into the brook that travels near;
Forthwith, that ancient Voice which Streams can hear
Thus speaks (that Voice which walks upon the wind,
Though seldom heard by busy human kind)--
"As thou these ashes, little Brook! wilt bear
"Into the Avon, Avon to the tide
"Of Severn, Severn to the narrow seas,
"Into main Ocean they, this deed accurst
"An emblem yields to friends and enemies
"How the bold Teacher's Doctrine, sanctified
"By truth, shall spread, throughout the world dispersed."

XVIII. CORRUPTIONS OF THE HIGHER CLERGY

"Woe to you, Prelates! rioting in ease
"And cumbrous wealth--the shame of your estate;
"You, on whose progress dazzling trains await
"Of pompous horses; whom vain titles please;
"Who will be served by others on their knees,
"Yet will yourselves to God no service pay;
"Pastors who neither take nor point the way
"To Heaven; for, either lost in vanities
"Ye have no skill to teach, or if ye know
"And speak the word----" Alas! of fearful things
'Tis the most fearful when the people's eye
Abuse hath cleared from vain imaginings;

And taught the general voice to prophesy
Of Justice armed, and Pride to be laid low.

XIX. ABUSE OF MONASTIC POWER

And what is Penance with her knotted thong;
Mortification with the shirt of hair,
Wan cheek, and knees indurated with prayer,
Vigils, and fastings rigorous as long;
If cloistered Avarice scruple not to wrong
The pious, humble, useful Secular,
And rob the people of his daily care,
Scorning that world whose blindness makes her strong?
Inversion strange! that, unto One who lives
For self, and struggles with himself alone,
The amplest share of heavenly favour gives;
That to a Monk allots, both in the esteem
Of God and man, place higher than to him
Who on the good of others builds his own!

XX. MONASTIC VOLUPTUOUSNESS

Yet more,--round many a Convent's blazing fire
Unhallowed threads of revelry are spun;
There Venus sits disguised like a Nun,--
While Bacchus, clothed in semblance of a Friar,
Pours out his choicest beverage high and higher
Sparkling, until it cannot choose but run
Over the bowl, whose silver lip hath won
An instant kiss of masterful desire--
To stay the precious waste. Through every brain
The domination of the sprightly juice
Spreads high conceits to madding Fancy dear,
Till the arched roof, with resolute abuse
Of its grave echoes, swells a choral strain,
Whose votive burthen is--"OUR KINGDOM'S HERE!"

XXI. DISSOLUTION OF THE MONASTERIES

Threats come which no submission may assuage,
No sacrifice avert, no power dispute;
The tapers shall be quenched, the belfries mute,

And, 'mid their choirs unroofed by selfish rage,
The warbling wren shall find a leafy cage;
The gadding bramble hang her purple fruit;
And the green lizard and the gilded newt
Lead unmolested lives, and die of age.
The owl of evening and the woodland fox
For their abode the shrines of Waltham choose:
Proud Glastonbury can no more refuse
To stoop her head before these desperate shocks--
She whose high pomp displaced, as story tells,
Arimathean Joseph's wattled cells.

XXII. THE SAME SUBJECT

The lovely Nun (submissive, but more meek
Through saintly habit than from effort due
To unrelenting mandates that pursue
With equal wrath the steps of strong and weak)
Goes forth unveiling timidly a cheek
Suffused with blushes of celestial hue,
While through the Convent's gate to open view
Softly she glides, another home to seek.
Not Iris, issuing from her cloudy shrine,
An Apparition more divinely bright!
Not more attractive to the dazzled sight
Those watery glories, on the stormy brine
Poured forth, while summer suns at distance shine,
And the green vales lie hushed in sober light!

XXIII. CONTINUED

Yet many a Novice of the cloistral shade,
And many chained by vows, with eager glee
The warrant hail, exulting to be free;
Like ships before whose keels, full long embayed
In polar ice, propitious winds have made
Unlooked-for outlet to an open sea,
Their liquid world, for bold discovery,
In all her quarters temptingly displayed!
Hope guides the young; but when the old must pass
The threshold, whither shall they turn to find
The hospitality--the alms (alas!
Alms may be needed) which that House bestowed?
Can they, in faith and worship, train the mind

To keep this new and questionable road?

XXIV. SAINTS

Ye, too, must fly before a chasing hand,
Angels and Saints, in every hamlet mourned!
Ah! if the old idolatry be spurned,
Let not your radiant Shapes desert the Land:
Her adoration was not your demand,
The fond heart proffered it--the servile heart;
And therefore are ye summoned to depart,
Michael, and thou, St. George, whose flaming brand
The Dragon quelled; and valiant Margaret
Whose rival sword a like Opponent slew:
And rapt Cecilia seraph-haunted Queen
Of harmony; and weeping Magdalene,
Who in the penitential desert met
Gales sweet as those that over Eden blew!

XXV. THE VIRGIN

Mother! whose virgin bosom was uncrost
With the least shade of thought to sin allied;
Woman! above all women glorified,
Our tainted nature's solitary boast;
Purer than foam on central ocean tost;
Brighter than eastern skies at daybreak strewn
With fancied roses, than the unblemished moon
Before her wane begins on heaven's blue coast;
Thy Image falls to earth. Yet some, I ween,
Not unforgiven the suppliant knee might bend,
As to a visible Power, in which did blend
All that was mixed and reconciled in Thee
Of mother's love with maiden purity,
Of high with low, celestial with terrene!

XXVI. APOLOGY

Not utterly unworthy to endure
Was the supremacy of crafty Rome;
Age after age to the arch of Christendom
Aerial keystone haughtily secure;

Supremacy from Heaven transmitted pure,
As many hold; and, therefore, to the tomb
Pass, some through fire--and by the scaffold some--
Like saintly Fisher, and unbending More.
"Lightly for both the bosom's lord did sit
"Upon his throne;" unsoftened, undismayed
By aught that mingled with the tragic scene
Of pity or fear: and More's gay genius played
With the inoffensive sword of native wit,
Than the bare axe more luminous and keen.

XXVII. IMAGINATIVE REGRETS

Deep is the lamentation! Not alone
From Sages justly honoured by mankind;
But from the ghostly tenants of the wind,
Demons and Spirits, many a dolorous groan
Issues for that dominion overthrown:
Proud Tiber grieves, and far-off Ganges, blind
As his own worshippers: and Nile, reclined
Upon his monstrous urn, the farewell moan
Renews. Through every forest, cave, and den,
Where frauds were hatched of old, hath sorrow past--
Hangs o'er the Arabian Prophet's native Waste,
Where once his airy helpers schemed and planned
'Mid spectral lakes bemocking thirsty men,
And stalking pillars built of fiery sand.

XXVIII. REFLECTIONS

Grant, that by this unsparing hurricane
Green leaves with yellow mixed are torn away,
And goodly fruitage with the mother spray;
'Twere madness--wished we, therefore, to detain,
With hands stretched forth in mollified disdain,
The "trumpery" that ascends in bare display--
Bulls, pardons, relics, cowls black, white, and grey--
Upwhirled, and flying o'er the ethereal plain
Fast bound for Limbo Lake. And yet not choice
But habit rules the unreflecting herd,
And airy bonds are hardest to disown;
Hence, with the spiritual sovereignty transferred
Unto itself, the Crown assumes a voice
Of reckless mastery, hitherto unknown.

XXX. THE POINT AT ISSUE

For what contend the wise?--for nothing less
Than that the Soul, freed from the bonds of Sense,
And to her God restored by evidence
Of things not seen, drawn forth from their recess,
Root there, and not in forms, her holiness;--
For Faith, which to the Patriarchs did dispense
Sure guidance, ere a ceremonial fence
Was needful round men thirsting to transgress;--
For Faith, more perfect still, with which the Lord
Of all, himself a Spirit, in the youth
Of Christian aspiration, deigned to fill
The temples of their hearts who, with his word
Informed, were resolute to do his will,
And worship him in spirit and in truth.

XXXI. EDWARD VI

"Sweet is the holiness of Youth"--so felt
Time-honoured Chaucer speaking through that Lay
By which the Prioress beguiled the way,
And many a Pilgrim's rugged heart did melt.
Hadst thou, loved Bard! whose spirit often dwelt
In the clear land of vision, but foreseen
King, child, and seraph, blended in the mien
Of pious Edward kneeling as he knelt
In meek and simple infancy, what joy
For universal Christendom had thrilled
Thy heart! what hopes inspired thy genius, skilled
(O great Precursor, genuine morning Star)
The lucid shafts of reason to employ,
Piercing the Papal darkness from afar!

XXXII. EDWARD SIGNING THE WARRANT FOR THE EXECUTION OF JOAN OF KENT

The tears of man in various measure gush
From various sources; gently overflow
From blissful transport some--from clefts of woe
Some with ungovernable impulse rush;
And some, coeval with the earliest blush

Of infant passion, scarcely dare to show
Their pearly lustre--coming but to go;
And some break forth when others' sorrows crush
The sympathising heart. Nor these, nor yet
The noblest drops to admiration known,
To gratitude, to injuries forgiven--
Claim Heaven's regard like waters that have wet
The innocent eyes of youthful Monarchs driven
To pen the mandates, nature doth disown.

XXXIII. REVIVAL OF POPERY

The saintly Youth has ceased to rule, discrowned
By unrelenting Death. O People keen
For change, to whom the new looks always green!
Rejoicing did they cast upon the ground
Their Gods of wood and stone; and, at the sound
Of counter-proclamation, now are seen,
(Proud triumph is it for a sullen Queen!)
Lifting them up, the worship to confound
Of the Most High. Again do they invoke
The Creature, to the Creature glory give;
Again with frankincense the altars smoke
Like those the Heathen served; and mass is sung;
And prayer, man's rational prerogative,
Runs through blind channels of an unknown tongue.

XXXIV. LATIMER AND RIDLEY

How fast the Marian death-list is unrolled!
See Latimer and Ridley in the might
Of Faith stand coupled for a common flight!
One (like those prophets whom God sent of old)
Transfigured, from this kindling hath foretold
A torch of inextinguishable light;
The Other gains a confidence as bold;
And thus they foil their enemy's despite.
The penal instruments, the shows of crime,
Are glorified while this once-mitred pair
Of saintly Friends the "murtherer's chain partake,
Corded, and burning at the social stake:"
Earth never witnessed object more sublime
In constancy, in fellowship more fair!

XXXV. CRANMER

Outstretching flameward his upbraided hand
(O God of mercy, may no earthly Seat
Of judgment such presumptuous doom repeat!)
Amid the shuddering throng doth Cranmer stand;
Firm as the stake to which with iron band
His frame is tied; firm from the naked feet
To the bare head. The victory is complete;
The shrouded Body to the Soul's command
Answers with more than Indian fortitude,
Through all her nerves with finer sense endued,
Till breath departs in blissful aspiration:
Then, 'mid the ghastly ruins of the fire,
Behold the unalterable heart entire,
Emblem of faith untouched, miraculous attestation!

XXXVI. GENERAL VIEW OF THE TROUBLES OF THE REFORMATION

Aid, glorious Martyrs, from your fields of light,
Our mortal ken! Inspire a perfect trust
(While we look round) that Heaven's decrees are just:
Which few can hold committed to a fight
That shows, ev'n on its better side, the might
Of proud Self-will, Rapacity, and Lust,
'Mid clouds enveloped of polemic dust,
Which showers of blood seem rather to incite
Than to allay. Anathemas are hurled
From both sides; veteran thunders (the brute test
Of truth) are met by fulminations new--
Tartarean flags are caught at, and unfurled--
Friends strike at friends--the flying shall pursue--
And Victory sickens, ignorant where to rest!

XXXVII. ENGLISH REFORMERS IN EXILE

Scattering, like birds escaped the fowler's net,
Some seek with timely flight a foreign strand;
Most happy, re-assembled in a land
By dauntless Luther freed, could they forget
Their Country's woes. But scarcely have they met,
Partners in faith, and brothers in distress,

Free to pour forth their common thankfulness,
Ere hope declines:--their union is beset
With speculative notions rashly sown,
Whence thickly-sprouting growth of poisonous weeds;
Their forms are broken staves; their passions, steeds
That master them. How enviably blest
Is he who can, by help of grace, enthrone
The peace of God within his single breast!

XXXVIII. ELIZABETH

Hail, Virgin Queen! o'er many an envious bar
Triumphant, snatched from many a treacherous wile!
All hail, sage Lady, whom a grateful Isle
Hath blest, respiring from that dismal war
Stilled by thy voice! But quickly from afar
Defiance breathes with more malignant aim;
And alien storms with home-bred ferments claim
Portentous fellowship. Her silver car,
By sleepless prudence ruled, glides slowly on;
Unhurt by violence, from menaced taint
Emerging pure, and seemingly more bright:
Ah! wherefore yields it to a foul constraint
Black as the clouds its beams dispersed, while shone,
By men and angels blest, the glorious light?

XXXIX. EMINENT REFORMERS

Methinks that I could trip o'er heaviest soil,
Light as a buoyant bark from wave to wave,
Were mine the trusty staff that JEWEL gave
To youthful HOOKER, in familiar style
The gift exalting, and with playful smile:
For thus equipped, and bearing on his head
The Donor's farewell blessing, can he dread
Tempest, or length of way, or weight of toil?--
More sweet than odours caught by him who sails
Near spicy shores of Araby the blest,
A thousand times more exquisitely sweet,
The freight of holy feeling which we meet,
In thoughtful moments, wafted by the gales
From fields where good men walk, or bowers wherein they rest.

XL. THE SAME

Holy and heavenly Spirits as they are,
Spotless in life, and eloquent as wise,
With what entire affection do they prize
Their Church reformed! labouring with earnest care
To baffle all that may her strength impair;
That Church, the unperverted Gospel's seat;
In their afflictions a divine retreat;
Source of their liveliest hope, and tenderest prayer!--
The truth exploring with an equal mind,
In doctrine and communion they have sought
Firmly between the two extremes to steer;
But theirs the wise man's ordinary lot--
To trace right courses for the stubborn blind,
And prophesy to ears that will not hear.

XLI. DISTRACTIONS

Men, who have ceased to reverence, soon defy,
Their forefathers; lo! sects are formed, and split
With morbid restlessness;--the ecstatic fit
Spreads wide; though special mysteries multiply,
'The Saints must govern', is their common cry;
And so they labour, deeming Holy Writ
Disgraced by aught that seems content to sit
Beneath the roof of settled Modesty.
The Romanist exults; fresh hope he draws
From the confusion, craftily incites
The overweening, personates the mad--
To heap disgust upon the worthier Cause:
Totters the Throne; the new-born Church is sad,
For every wave against her peace unites.

XLII. GUNPOWDER PLOT

Fear hath a hundred eyes that all agree
To plague her beating heart; and there is one
(Nor idlest that!) which holds communion
With things that were not, yet were 'meant' to be.
Aghast within its gloomy cavity
That eye (which sees as if fulfilled and done
Crimes that might stop the motion of the sun)

Beholds the horrible catastrophe
Of an assembled Senate unredeemed
From subterraneous Treason's darkling power:
Merciless act of sorrow infinite!
Worse than the product of that dismal night,
When gushing, copious as a thunder-shower,
The blood of Huguenots through Paris streamed.

XLIII. THE JUNG-FRAU AND THE FALL OF THE RHINE NEAR SCHAFFHAUSEN

The Virgin Mountain, wearing like a Queen
A brilliant crown of everlasting snow,
Sheds ruin from her sides; and men below
Wonder that aught of aspect so serene
Can link with desolation. Smooth and green,
And seeming, at a little distance, slow,
The waters of the Rhine; but on they go
Fretting and whitening, keener and more keen;
Till madness seizes on the whole wide Flood,
Turned to a fearful Thing whose nostrils breathe
Blasts of tempestuous smoke--wherewith he tries
To hide himself, but only magnifies;
And doth in more conspicuous torment writhe,
Deafening the region in his ireful mood.

XLIV. TROUBLES OF CHARLES THE FIRST

Even such the contrast that, where'er we move,
To the mind's eye Religion doth present;
Now with her own deep quietness content;
Then, like the mountain, thundering from above
Against the ancient pine-trees of the grove
And the Land's humblest comforts. Now her mood
Recalls the transformation of the flood,
Whose rage the gentle skies in vain reprove;
Earth cannot check. O terrible excess
Of headstrong will! Can this be Piety?
No--some fierce Maniac hath usurped her name;
And scourges England struggling to be free:
Her peace destroyed! her hopes a wilderness!
Her blessings cursed--her glory turned to shame!

XLV. LAUD

Prejudged by foes determined not to spare,
An old weak Man for vengeance thrown aside,
Laud, "in the painful art of dying" tried,
(Like a poor bird entangled in a snare
Whose heart still flutters, though his wings forbear
To stir in useless struggle) hath relied
On hope that conscious innocence supplied,
And in his prison breathes celestial air.
Why tarries then thy chariot? Wherefore stay,
O Death! the ensanguined yet triumphant wheels,
Which thou prepar'st, full often, to convey
(What time a State with madding faction reels)
The Saint or Patriot to the world that heals
All wounds, all perturbations doth allay?

XLVI. AFFLICTIONS OF ENGLAND

Harp! could'st thou venture, on thy boldest string,
The faintest note to echo which the blast
Caught from the hand of Moses as it passed
O'er Sinai's top, or from the Shepherd-king,
Early awake, by Siloa's brook, to sing
Of dread Jehovah; then, should wood and waste
Hear also of that name, and mercy cast
Off to the mountains, like a covering
Of which the Lord was weary. Weep, oh! weep,
Weep with the good, beholding King and Priest
Despised by that stern God to whom they raise
Their suppliant hands; but holy is the feast
He keepeth; like the firmament his ways:
His statutes like the chambers of the deep.

PART III.

FROM THE RESTORATION TO THE PRESENT TIMES

I

I saw the figure of a lovely Maid
Seated alone beneath a darksome tree,
Whose fondly-overhanging canopy
Set off her brightness with a pleasing shade.

No Spirit was she; 'that' my heart betrayed,
For she was one I loved exceedingly;
But while I gazed in tender reverie
(Or was it sleep that with my Fancy played?)
The bright corporeal presence--form and face--
Remaining still distinct grew thin and rare,
Like sunny mist;--at length the golden hair,
Shape, limbs, and heavenly features, keeping pace
Each with the other in a lingering race
Of dissolution, melted into air.

II. PATRIOTIC SYMPATHIES

Last night, without a voice, that Vision spake
Fear to my Soul, and sadness which might seem
Wholly dissevered from our present theme;
Yet, my beloved Country! I partake
Of kindred agitations for thy sake;
Thou, too, dost visit oft my midnight dream;
Thy glory meets me with the earliest beam
Of light, which tells that Morning is awake.
If aught impair thy beauty or destroy,
Or but forebode destruction, I deplore
With filial love the sad vicissitude;
If thou hast fallen, and righteous Heaven restore
The prostrate, then my spring-time is renewed,
And sorrow bartered for exceeding joy.

III. CHARLES THE SECOND

Who comes--with rapture greeted, and caressed
With frantic love--his kingdom to regain?
Him Virtue's Nurse, Adversity, in vain
Received, and fostered in her iron breast:
For all she taught of hardiest and of best,
Or would have taught, by discipline of pain
And long privation, now dissolves amain,
Or is remembered only to give zest
To wantonness.--Away, Circean revels!
But for what gain? if England soon must sink
Into a gulf which all distinction levels
That bigotry may swallow the good name,
And, with that draught, the life-blood: misery, shame,
By Poets loathed; from which Historians shrink!

IV. LATITUDINARIANISM

Yet Truth is keenly sought for, and the wind
Charged with rich words poured out in thought's defence;
Whether the Church inspire that eloquence,
Or a Platonic Piety confined
To the sole temple of the inward mind;
And One there is who builds immortal lays,
Though doomed to tread in solitary ways,
Darkness before and danger's voice behind;
Yet not alone, nor helpless to repel
Sad thoughts; for from above the starry sphere
Come secrets, whispered nightly to his ear;
And the pure spirit of celestial light
Shines through his soul--"that he may see and tell
Of things invisible to mortal sight."

V. WALTON'S BOOK OF LIVES

There are no colours in the fairest sky
So fair as these. The feather, whence the pen
Was shaped that traced the lives of these good men,
Dropped from an Angel's wing. With moistened eye
We read of faith and purest charity
In Statesman, Priest, and humble Citizen:
Oh could we copy their mild virtues, then
What joy to live, what blessedness to die!
Methinks their very names shine still and bright;
Apart--like glow-worms on a summer night;
Or lonely tapers when from far they fling
A guiding ray; or seen--like stars on high,
Satellites burning in a lucid ring
Around meek Walton's heavenly memory.

VI. CLERICAL INTEGRITY

Nor shall the eternal roll of praise reject
Those Unconforming; whom one rigorous day
Drives from their Cures, a voluntary prey
To poverty, and grief, and disrespect.
And some to want--as if by tempests wrecked

On a wild coast how destitute! did They
Feel not that Conscience never can betray,
That peace of mind is Virtue's sure effect.
Their altars they forego, their homes they quit,
Fields which they love, and paths they daily trod,
And cast the future upon Providence;
As men the dictate of whose inward sense
Outweighs the world; whom self-deceiving wit
Lures not from what they deem the cause of God.

VII. PERSECUTION OF THE SCOTTISH COVENANTERS

When Alpine Vales threw forth a suppliant cry,
The Majesty of England interposed
And the sword stopped; the bleeding wounds were closed;
And Faith preserved her ancient purity.
How little boots that precedent of good,
Scorned or forgotten, Thou canst testify,
For England's shame, O Sister Realm! from wood,
Mountain, and moor, and crowded street, where lie
The headless martyrs of the Covenant,
Slain by Compatriot-protestants that draw
From councils senseless as intolerant
Their warrant. Bodies fall by wild sword-law;
But who would force the Soul, tilts with a straw
Against a Champion cased in adamant.

VIII. ACQUITTAL OF THE BISHOPS

A voice, from long-expecting thousands sent,
Shatters the air, and troubles tower and spire;
For Justice hath absolved the innocent,
And Tyranny is balked of her desire:
Up, down, the busy Thames--rapid as fire
Coursing a train of gunpowder--it went,
And transport finds in every street a vent,
Till the whole City rings like one vast quire.
The Fathers urge the People to be still,
With outstretched hands and earnest speech--in vain!
Yea, many, haply wont to entertain
Small reverence for the mitre's offices,
And to Religion's self no friendly will,
A Prelate's blessing ask on bended knees.

IX. WILLIAM THE THIRD

Calm as an under-current, strong to draw
Millions of waves into itself, and run,
From sea to sea, impervious to the sun
And ploughing storm, the spirit of Nassau
Swerves not, (how blest if by religious awe
Swayed, and thereby enabled to contend
With the wide world's commotions) from its end
Swerves not--diverted by a casual law.
Had mortal action e'er a nobler scope?
The Hero comes to liberate, not defy;
And, while he marches on with stedfast hope,
Conqueror beloved! expected anxiously!
The vacillating Bondman of the Pope
Shrinks from the verdict of his stedfast eye.

X. OBLIGATIONS OF CIVIL TO RELIGIOUS LIBERTY

Ungrateful Country, if thou e'er forget
The sons who for thy civil rights have bled!
How, like a Roman, Sidney bowed his head,
And Russel's milder blood the scaffold wet;
But these had fallen for profitless regret
Had not thy holy Church her champions bred,
And claims from other worlds inspirited
The star of Liberty to rise. Nor yet
(Grave this within thy heart!) if spiritual things
Be lost, through apathy, or scorn, or fear,
Shalt thou thy humbler franchises support,
However hardly won or justly dear:
What came from heaven to heaven by nature clings,
And, if dissevered thence, its course is short.

XI. SACHEVEREL

A sudden conflict rises from the swell
Of a proud slavery met by tenets strained
In Liberty's behalf. Fears, true or feigned,
Spread through all ranks; and lo! the Sentinel
Who loudest rang his pulpit 'larum bell,
Stands at the Bar, absolved by female eyes
Mingling their glances with grave flatteries

Lavished on 'Him'--that England may rebel
Against her ancient virtue. HIGH and LOW,
Watchwords of Party, on all tongues are rife;
As if a Church, though sprung from heaven, must owe
To opposites and fierce extremes her life,--
Not to the golden mean, and quiet flow
Of truths that soften hatred, temper strife.

XII

Down a swift Stream, thus far, a bold design
Have we pursued, with livelier stir of heart
Than his who sees, borne forward by the Rhine,
The living landscapes greet him, and depart;
Sees spires fast sinking--up again to start!
And strives the towers to number, that recline
O'er the dark steeps, or on the horizon line
Striding with shattered crests his eye athwart,
So have we hurried on with troubled pleasure:
Henceforth, as on the bosom of a stream
That slackens, and spreads wide a watery gleam,
We, nothing loth a lingering course to measure,
May gather up our thoughts, and mark at leisure
How widely spread the interests of our theme.

XIII. ASPECTS OF CHRISTIANITY IN AMERICA

I. THE PILGRIM FATHERS

Well worthy to be magnified are they
Who, with sad hearts, of friends and country took
A last farewell, their loved abodes forsook,
And hallowed ground in which their fathers lay;
Then to the new-found World explored their way,
That so a Church, unforced, uncalled to brook
Ritual restraints, within some sheltering nook
Her Lord might worship and his word obey
In freedom. Men they were who could not bend;
Blest Pilgrims, surely, as they took for guide
A will by sovereign Conscience sanctified;
Blest while their Spirits from the woods ascend
Along a Galaxy that knows no end,
But in His glory who for Sinners died.

XIV

II. CONTINUED

From Rite and Ordinance abused they fled
To Wilds where both were utterly unknown;
But not to them had Providence foreshown
What benefits are missed, what evils bred,
In worship neither raised nor limited
Save by Self-will. Lo! from that distant shore,
For Rite and Ordinance, Piety is led
Back to the Land those Pilgrims left of yore,
Led by her own free choice. So Truth and Love
By Conscience governed do their steps retrace.--
Fathers! your Virtues, such the power of grace,
Their spirit, in your Children, thus approve.
Transcendent over time, unbound by place,
Concord and Charity in circles move.

XV

III. CONCLUDED.--AMERICAN EPISCOPACY

Patriots informed with Apostolic light
Were they, who, when their Country had been freed,
Bowing with reverence to the ancient creed,
Fixed on the frame of England's Church their sight,
And strove in filial love to reunite
What force had severed. Thence they fetched the seed
Of Christian unity, and won a meed
Of praise from Heaven. To Thee, O saintly WHITE,
Patriarch of a wide-spreading family,
Remotest lands and unborn times shall turn,
Whether they would restore or build--to Thee,
As one who rightly taught how zeal should burn,
As one who drew from out Faith's holiest urn
The purest stream of patient Energy.

XVI

Bishops and Priests, blessed are ye, if deep
(As yours above all offices is high)
Deep in your hearts the sense of duty lie;

Charged as ye are by Christ to feed and keep
From wolves your portion of his chosen sheep:
Labouring as ever in your Master's sight,
Making your hardest task your best delight,
What perfect glory ye in Heaven shall reap!--
But, in the solemn Office which ye sought
And undertook premonished, if unsound
Your practice prove, faithless though but in thought,
Bishops and Priests, think what a gulf profound
Awaits yon then, if they were rightly taught
Who framed the Ordinance by your lives disowned!

XVII. PLACES OF WORSHIP

As star that shines dependent upon star
Is to the sky while we look up and love;
As to the deep fair ships which though they move
Seem fixed, to eyes that watch them from afar;
As to the sandy desert fountains are,
With palm-groves shaded at wide intervals,
Whose fruit around the sun-burnt Native falls
Of roving tired or desultory war--
Such to this British Isle her christian Fanes,
Each linked to each for kindred services;
Her Spires, her Steeple-towers with glittering vanes
Far-kenned, her Chapels lurking among trees,
Where a few villagers on bended knees
Find solace which a busy world disdains.

XVIII. PASTORAL CHARACTER

A genial hearth, a hospitable board,
And a refined rusticity, belong
To the neat mansion, where, his flock among,
The learned Pastor dwells, their watchful Lord.
Though meek and patient as a sheathed sword;
Though pride's least lurking thought appear a wrong
To human kind; though peace be on his tongue,
Gentleness in his heart--can earth afford
Such genuine state, pre-eminence so free,
As when, arrayed in Christ's authority,
He from the pulpit lifts his awful hand;
Conjures, implores, and labours all he can
For re-subjecting to divine command

The stubborn spirit of rebellious man?

XIX. THE LITURGY

Yes, if the intensities of hope and fear
Attract us still, and passionate exercise
Of lofty thoughts, the way before us lies
Distinct with signs, through which in set career,
As through a zodiac, moves the ritual year
Of England's Church; stupendous mysteries!
Which whoso travels in her bosom eyes,
As he approaches them, with solemn cheer.
Upon that circle traced from sacred story
We only dare to cast a transient glance,
Trusting in hope that Others may advance
With mind intent upon the King of Glory,
From his mild advent till his countenance
Shall dissipate the seas and mountains hoary.

XX. BAPTISM

Dear be the Church, that, watching o'er the needs
Of Infancy, provides a timely shower
Whose virtue changes to a christian Flower
A Growth from sinful Nature's bed of weeds!--
Fitliest beneath the sacred roof proceeds
The ministration; while parental Love
Looks on, and Grace descendeth from above
As the high service pledges now, now pleads.
There, should vain thoughts outspread their wings and fly
To meet the coming hours of festal mirth,
The tombs--which hear and answer that brief cry,
The Infant's notice of his second birth--
Recall the wandering Soul to sympathy
With what man hopes from Heaven, yet fears from Earth.

XXI. SPONSORS

Father!--to God himself we cannot give
A holier name! then lightly do not bear
Both names conjoined, but of thy spiritual care
Be duly mindful: still more sensitive

Do Thou, in truth a second Mother, strive
Against disheartening custom, that by Thee
Watched, and with love and pious industry
Tended at need, the adopted Plant may thrive
For everlasting bloom. Benign and pure
This Ordinance, whether, loss it would supply,
Prevent omission, help deficiency,
Or seek to make assurance doubly sure.
Shame if the consecrated Vow be found
An idle form, the Word an empty sound!

XXII. CATECHISING

From Little down to Least, in due degree,
Around the Pastor, each in new-wrought vest,
Each with a vernal posy at his breast,
We stood, a trembling, earnest Company!
With low soft murmur, like a distant bee,
Some spake, by thought-perplexing fears betrayed,
And some a bold unerring answer made:
How fluttered then thy anxious heart for me,
Beloved Mother! Thou whose happy hand
Had bound the flowers I wore, with faithful tie:
Sweet flowers! at whose inaudible command
Her countenance, phantom-like, doth reappear:
O lost too early for the frequent tear,
And ill requited by this heartfelt sigh!

XXIII. CONFIRMATION

The Young-ones gathered in from hill and dale,
With holiday delight on every brow:
'Tis passed away; far other thoughts prevail;
For they are taking the baptismal Vow
Upon their conscious selves; their own lips speak
The solemn promise. Strongest sinews fail,
And many a blooming, many a lovely, cheek
Under the holy fear of God turns pale;
While on each head his lawn-robed Servant lays
An apostolic hand, and with prayer seals
The Covenant. The Omnipotent will raise
Their feeble Souls; and bear with 'his' regrets,
Who, looking round the fair assemblage, feels
That ere the Sun goes down their childhood sets.

XXIV. CONFIRMATION CONTINUED

I saw a Mother's eye intensely bent
Upon a Maiden trembling as she knelt;
In and for whom the pious Mother felt
Things that we judge of by a light too faint:
Tell, if ye may, some star-crowned Muse, or Saint!
Tell what rushed in, from what she was relieved--
Then, when her Child the hallowing touch received,
And such vibration through the Mother went
That tears burst forth amain. Did gleams appear?
Opened a vision of that blissful place
Where dwells a Sister-child? And was power given
Part of her lost One's glory back to trace
Even to this Rite? For thus 'She' knelt, and, ere
The summer-leaf had faded, passed to Heaven.

XXV. SACRAMENT

By chain yet stronger must the Soul be tied:
One duty more, last stage of this ascent,
Brings to thy food, mysterious Sacrament!
The Offspring, haply, at the Parent's side;
But not till They, with all that do abide
In Heaven, have lifted up their hearts to laud
And magnify the glorious name of God,
Fountain of grace, whose Son for sinners died.
Ye, who have duly weighed the summons, pause
No longer; ye, whom to the saving rite
The Altar calls, come early under laws
That can secure for you a path of light
Through gloomiest shade; put on (nor dread its weight)
Armour divine, and conquer in your cause!

XXVI. THE MARRIAGE CEREMONY

The Vested Priest before the Altar stands;
Approach, come gladly, ye prepared, in sight
Of God and chosen friends, your troth to plight
With the symbolic ring, and willing hands
Solemnly joined. Now sanctify the bands

O Father!--to the Espoused thy blessing give,
That mutually assisted they may live
Obedient, as here taught, to thy commands.
So prays the Church, to consecrate a Vow
"The which would endless matrimony make;"
Union that shadows forth and doth partake
A mystery potent human love to endow
With heavenly, each more prized for the other's sake;
Weep not, meek Bride! uplift thy timid brow.

XXVII. THANKSGIVING AFTER CHILDBIRTH

Woman! the Power who left his throne on high,
And deigned to wear the robe of flesh we wear,
The Power that thro' the straits of Infancy
Did pass dependent on maternal care,
His own humanity with Thee will share,
Pleased with the thanks that in his People's eye
Thou offerest up for safe Delivery
From Childbirth's perilous throes. And should the Heir
Of thy fond hopes hereafter walk inclined
To courses fit to make a mother rue
That ever he was born, a glance of mind
Cast upon this observance may renew
A better will; and, in the imagined view
Of thee thus kneeling, safety he may find.

XXVIII. VISITATION OF THE SICK

The Sabbath bells renew the inviting peal;
Glad music! yet there be that, worn with pain
And sickness, listen where they long have lain,
In sadness listen. With maternal zeal
Inspired, the Church sends ministers to kneel
Beside the afflicted; to sustain with prayer,
And soothe the heart confession hath laid bare--
That pardon, from God's throne, may set its seal
On a true Penitent. When breath departs
From one disburthened so, so comforted,
His Spirit Angels greet; and ours be hope
That, if the Sufferer rise from his sick-bed,
Hence he will gain a firmer mind, to cope
With a bad world, and foil the Tempter's arts.

XXIX. THE COMMINATION SERVICE

Shun not this Rite, neglected, yea abhorred,
By some of unreflecting mind, as calling
Man to curse man, (thought monstrous and appalling.)
Go thou and hear the threatenings of the LORD;
Listening within his Temple see his sword
Unsheathed in wrath to strike the offender's head,
Thy own, if sorrow for thy sin be dead,
Guilt unrepented, pardon unimplored.
Two aspects bears Truth needful for salvation;
Who knows not 'that?'--yet would this delicate age
Look only on the Gospel's brighter page:
Let light and dark duly our thoughts employ;
So shall the fearful words of Commination
Yield timely fruit of peace and love and joy.

XXX. FORMS OF PRAYER AT SEA

To kneeling Worshippers no earthly floor
Gives holier invitation than the deck
Of a storm-shattered Vessel saved from Wreck
(When all that Man could do availed no more)
By him who raised the Tempest and restrains:
Happy the crew who this have felt, and pour
Forth for his mercy, as the Church ordains,
Solemn thanksgiving. Nor will 'they' implore
In vain who, for a rightful cause, give breath
To words the Church prescribes aiding the lip
For the heart's sake, ere ship with hostile ship
Encounters, armed for work of pain and death.
Suppliants! the God to whom your cause ye trust
Will listen, and ye know that He is just.

XXXI. FUNERAL SERVICE

From the Baptismal hour, thro' weal and woe,
The Church extends her care to thought and deed;
Nor quits the Body when the Soul is freed,
The mortal weight cast off to be laid low.
Blest Rite for him who hears in faith, "I know
That my Redeemer liveth,"--hears each word

That follows--striking on some kindred chord
Deep in the thankful heart;--yet tears will flow.
Man is as grass that springeth up at morn,
Grows green, and is cut down and withereth
Ere nightfall--truth that well may claim a sigh,
Its natural echo; but hope comes reborn
At Jesu's bidding. We rejoice, "O Death,
Where is thy Sting?--O Grave, where is thy Victory?"

XXII. RURAL CEREMONY

Closing the sacred Book which long has fed
Our meditations, give we to a day
Of annual joy one tributary lay;
This day, when, forth by rustic music led,
The village Children, while the sky is red
With evening lights, advance in long array
Through the still churchyard, each with garland gay,
That, carried sceptre-like, o'ertops the head
Of the proud Bearer. To the wide church-door,
Charged with these offerings which their fathers bore
For decoration in the Papal time,
The innocent procession softly moves:--
The spirit of Laud is pleased in heaven's pure clime,
And Hooker's voice the spectacle approves!

XXXIII. REGRETS

Would that our scrupulous Sires had dared to leave
Less scanty measure of those graceful rites
And usages, whose due return invites
A stir of mind too natural to deceive;
Giving to Memory help when she would weave
A crown for Hope!--I dread the boasted lights
That all too often are but fiery blights,
Killing the bud o'er which in vain we grieve.
Go, seek, when Christmas snows discomfort bring,
The counter Spirit found in some gay church
Green with fresh holly, every pew a perch
In which the linnet or the thrush might sing,
Merry and loud and safe from prying search,
Strains offered only to the genial Spring.

XXXIV. MUTABILITY

From low to high doth dissolution climb,
And sink from high to low, along a scale
Of awful notes, whose concord shall not fail;
A musical but melancholy chime,
Which they can hear who meddle not with crime,
Nor avarice, nor over-anxious care.
Truth fails not; but her outward forms that bear
The longest date do melt like frosty rime,
That in the morning whitened hill and plain
And is no more; drop like the tower sublime
Of yesterday, which royally did wear
His crown of weeds, but could not even sustain
Some casual shout that broke the silent air,
Or the unimaginable touch of Time.

XXXV. OLD ABBEYS

Monastic Domes! following my downward way,
Untouched by due regret I marked your fall!
Now, ruin, beauty, ancient stillness, all
Dispose to judgments temperate as we lay
On our past selves in life's declining day:
For as, by discipline of Time made wise,
We learn to tolerate the infirmities
And faults of others--gently as he may,
So with our own the mild Instructor deals,
Teaching us to forget them or forgive.
Perversely curious, then, for hidden ill
Why should we break Time's charitable seals?
Once ye were holy, ye are holy still;
Your spirit freely let me drink, and live!

XXXVI. EMIGRANT FRENCH CLERGY

Even while I speak, the sacred roofs of France
Are shattered into dust; and self-exiled
From altars threatened, levelled, or defiled,
Wander the Ministers of God, as chance
Opens a way for life, or consonance
Of faith invites. More welcome to no land
The fugitives than to the British strand,

Where priest and layman with the vigilance
Of true compassion greet them. Creed and test
Vanish before the unreserved embrace
Of catholic humanity:--distrest
They came,--and, while the moral tempest roars
Throughout the Country they have left, our shores
Give to their Faith a fearless resting-place.

XXXVII. CONGRATULATION

Thus all things lead to Charity secured
By THEM who blessed the soft and happy gale
That landward urged the great Deliverer's sail,
Till in the sunny bay his fleet was moored!
Propitious hour!--had we, like them, endured
Sore stress of apprehension, with a mind
Sickened by injuries, dreading worse designed,
From month to month trembling and unassured,
How had we then rejoiced! But we have felt,
As a loved substance, their futurity:
Good, which they dared not hope for, we have seen;
A State whose generous will through earth is dealt;
A State--which, balancing herself between
Licence and slavish order, dares be free.

XXXVIII. NEW CHURCHES

But liberty, and triumphs on the Main,
And laurelled armies, not to be withstood--
What serve they? if, on transitory good
Intent, and sedulous of abject gain,
The State (ah, surely not preserved in vain!)
Forbear to shape due channels which the Flood
Of sacred truth may enter--till it brood
O'er the wide realm, as o'er the Egyptian plain
The all-sustaining Nile. No more--the time
Is conscious of her want; through England's bounds,
In rival haste, the wished-for Temples rise!
I hear their sabbath bells' harmonious chime
Float on the breeze--the heavenliest of all sounds
That vale or hill prolongs or multiplies!

XXXIX. CHURCH TO BE ERECTED

Be this the chosen site; the virgin sod,
Moistened from age to age by dewy eve,
Shall disappear, and grateful earth receive
The corner-stone from hands that build to God.
Yon reverend hawthorns, hardened to the rod
Of winter storms, yet budding cheerfully;
Those forest oaks of Druid memory,
Shall long survive, to shelter the Abode
Of genuine Faith. Where, haply, 'mid this band
Of daisies, shepherds sate of yore and wove
May-garlands, there let the holy altar stand
For kneeling adoration;--while--above,
Broods, visibly portrayed, the mystic Dove,
That shall protect from blasphemy the Land.

XL. CONTINUED

Mine ear has rung, my spirit sunk subdued,
Sharing the strong emotion of the crowd,
When each pale brow to dread hosannas bowed
While clouds of incense mounting veiled the rood,
That glimmered like a pine-tree dimly viewed
Through Alpine vapours. Such appalling rite
Our Church prepares not, trusting to the might
Of simple truth with grace divine imbued;
Yet will we not conceal the precious Cross,
Like men ashamed: the Sun with his first smile
Shall greet that symbol crowning the low Pile:
And the fresh air of incense-breathing morn
Shall wooingly embrace it; and green moss
Creep round its arms through centuries unborn.

XLI. NEW CHURCHYARD

The encircling ground, in native turf arrayed,
Is now by solemn consecration given
To social interests, and to favouring Heaven;
And where the rugged colts their gambols played,
And wild deer bounded through the forest glade,
Unchecked as when by merry Outlaw driven,
Shall hymns of praise resound at morn and even;
And soon, full soon, the lonely Sexton's spade

Shall wound the tender sod. Encincture small,
But infinite its grasp of weal and woe!
Hopes, fears, in never-ending ebb and flow;--
The spousal trembling, and the "dust to dust,"
The prayers, the contrite struggle, and the trust
That to the Almighty Father looks through all.

XLII. CATHEDRALS, ETC.

Open your gates, ye everlasting Piles!
Types of the spiritual Church which God hath reared;
Not loth we quit the newly-hallowed sward
And humble altar, 'mid your sumptuous aisles
To kneel, or thrid your intricate defiles,
Or down the nave to pace in motion slow;
Watching, with upward eye, the tall tower grow
And mount, at every step, with living wiles
Instinct--to rouse the heart and lead the will
By a bright ladder to the world above.
Open your gates, ye Monuments of love
Divine! thou Lincoln, on thy sovereign hill!
Thou, stately York! and Ye, whose splendours cheer
Isis and Cam, to patient Science dear!

XLIII. INSIDE OF KING'S COLLEGE CHAPEL, CAMBRIDGE

Tax not the royal Saint with vain expense,
With ill-matched alms the Architect who planned--
Albeit labouring for a scanty band
Of white robed Scholars only--this immense
And glorious Work of fine intelligence!
Give all thou canst; high Heaven rejects the lore
Of nicely-calculated less or more;
So deemed the man who fashioned for the sense
These lofty pillars, spread that branching roof
Self-poised, and scooped into ten thousand cells,
Where light and shade repose, where music dwells
Lingering--and wandering on as loth to die;
Like thoughts whose very sweetness yieldeth proof
That they were born for immortality.

XLIV. THE SAME

What awful perspective! while from our sight
With gradual stealth the lateral windows hide
Their Portraitures, their stone-work glimmers, dyed
In the soft chequerings of a sleepy light.
Martyr, or King, or sainted Eremite,
Whoe'er ye be, that thus, yourselves unseen,
Imbue your prison-bars with solemn sheen,
Shine on, until ye fade with coming Night!--
But, from the arms of silence--list! O list!
The music bursteth into second life;
The notes luxuriate, every stone is kissed
By sound, or ghost of sound, in mazy strife;
Heart-thrilling strains, that cast, before the eye
Of the devout, a veil of ecstasy!

XLV. CONTINUED

They dreamt not of a perishable home
Who thus could build. Be mine, in hours of fear
Or grovelling thought, to seek a refuge here;
Or through the aisles of Westminster to roam:
Where bubbles burst, and folly's dancing foam
Melts, if it cross the threshold; where the wreath
Of awe-struck wisdom droops: or let my path
Lead to that younger Pile, whose sky-like dome
Hath typified by reach of daring art
Infinity's embrace; whose guardian crest,
The silent Cross, among the stars shall spread
As now, when She hath also seen her breast
Filled with mementos, satiate with its part
Of grateful England's overflowing Dead.

XLVI. EJACULATION

Glory to God! and to the Power who came
In filial duty, clothed with love divine,
That made his human tabernacle shine
Like Ocean burning with purpureal flame;
Or like the Alpine Mount, that takes its name
From roseate hues, far kenned at morn and even
In hours of peace, or when the storm is driven
Along the nether region's rugged frame!
Earth prompts--Heaven urges; let us seek the light,

Studious of that pure intercourse begun
When first our infant brows their lustre won;
So, like the Mountain, may we grow more bright
From unimpeded commerce with the Sun,
At the approach of all-involving night.

XLVII. CONCLUSION

Why sleeps the future, as a snake enrolled,
Coil within coil, at noon-tide? For the WORD
Yields, if with unpresumptuous faith explored,
Power at whose touch the sluggard shall unfold
His drowsy rings. Look forth!--that Stream behold,
THAT STREAM upon whose bosom we have passed
Floating at ease while nations have effaced
Nations, and Death has gathered to his fold
Long lines of mighty Kings--look forth, my Soul!
(Nor in this vision be thou slow to trust)
The living Waters, less and less by guilt
Stained and polluted, brighten as they roll,
Till they have reached the eternal City--built
For the perfected Spirit of the just!

William Wordsworth – A Short Biography

William Wordsworth was born on 7 April, 1770 in Cockermouth, in Cumbria, northwest England.

A poet of world class stature and authority his initial introduction to poetry came from his father, John Wordsworth. But his frequent absences meant that William was essentially raised by his Mother's parents in Penrith and these times were endured by William as a painful period of conflict and dark thoughts of suicide.

But the landscape surrounding him did eventually seep into him and he would walk for many hours in the fells of the Lake District often with his sister, Dorothy, to whom he was increasingly attached.

In 1778, the young William was sent to Hawkshead Grammar School in Lancashire; he was to now be separated from Dorothy for nine years. At Hawkshead he received an excellent education encompassing classics, literature, and mathematics, but for him there was the greater education to indulge in; the boyhood pleasures of living and playing in the outdoors. The natural scenery of the English lakes could terrify as well as nurture, as Wordsworth would write "I grew up fostered alike by beauty and by fear,"

By 1787, he had arrived at St. John's College, Cambridge and also to publish his first poem, a sonnet for the European magazine. But he distanced himself from the competitive pressures of University life and idled his way through saying he "was not for that hour, nor for that place."

In 1790, whilst still at Cambridge he travelled to France. He was immediately taken by the Revolutionary fervor and the confluence of a set of great ideals and rallying calls for the people of France.

Upon taking his Cambridge degree, an un-ambitious "pass", he returned in 1791 to France, where he met and began an affair with Annette Vallon. Their illegitimate child, Anne Caroline, was born in December 1792. Wordsworth wanted to marry but returned alone to England. The beginning of hostilities between England and France meant he would not see his daughter until she was nine but he maintained his financial obligations to his daughter whilst keeping her hidden from the public gaze.

For Wordsworth this blow was compounded by the 'Reign of Terror' and its trampling upon the ideals of 'liberté, égalité, fraternité'.

There now followed a period of three to four years that plagued Wordsworth with doubt. He was now in his early thirties but had no profession, was rootless and virtually penniless as well as being totally opposed to his country's position on the French. He lived in London with radicals such as William Godwin and felt profound sympathy for the abandoned mothers, beggars, children, vagrants, and victims of England's wars who began to take form in the darker, more melancholy poems he began writing at this time.

Although his career was not on track he did manage to publish two volumes, both in 1793; An Evening Walk and Descriptive Sketches.

This dark period ended in 1795. A legacy of £900 received from Raisley Calvert enabled Wordsworth to pursue a literary career in earnest.

This bequest almost made possible a reunion with his beloved sister Dorothy. They were never to be apart again and they moved in 1797 to Alfoxden House, near Bristol.

It was here that Wordsworth now became great friends with a fellow poet, Samuel Taylor Coleridge. They formed a partnership that would change both their lives and the course of English poetry.

This next year when Wordsworth and Coleridge were "together wantoned in wild Poesy," had two direct results for Wordsworth. Firstly he moved away from the long poems he had been laboring upon; these included poems of social protest like Salisbury Plain, loco-descriptive poems such as An Evening Walk and Descriptive Sketches, and The Borderers, a blank-verse tragedy exploring the psychology of guilt (published only in 1842).

Emboldened by Coleridge and under the marveling influences of nature and his sister, Wordsworth began to write the short lyrical and dramatic poems for which he is best remembered.

The aim of much of these short works was to provide a decisive break with the strictures of Neoclassical verse. They first appeared in 1798 in a slim, anonymously authored volume entitled Lyrical Ballads. Wordsworth wrote in the preface "the spontaneous overflow of powerful feelings: it takes its origin from emotion recollected in tranquility." The book began with Coleridge's long poem "The Rime of the Ancient Mariner" and ended with Wordsworth's "Tintern Abbey."

All but three of the other poems were written by Wordsworth. Two years later in a preface to a second edition he wrote that their objective was "to choose incidents and situations from common life and to relate or describe them...in a selection of language really used by men...tracing in them...the primary laws of our nature."

Most of the poems were dramatic in form, designed to reveal the character of the speaker. Thus the poems set forth a new style, a new vocabulary, and new subjects for poetry.

The second consequence of Wordsworth's work with Coleridge was the structuring of a vastly ambitious poetic design that teased and haunted him for the rest of his life.

Coleridge had conceived of an enormous poem to be called "The Brook," in which he proposed to treat all science, philosophy, and religion, but he soon laid the burden of writing this poem upon Wordsworth himself.

As early as 1798 Wordsworth began to talk in grand terms of this poem, to be entitled The Recluse. To nerve himself up to this enterprise and to test his powers, Wordsworth began writing the autobiographical poem that would absorb him intermittently for the next 40 years, and which was eventually published in 1850 under the title The Prelude, or, Growth of a Poet's Mind.

The Recluse itself was never completed; only one of its three parts was actually written; this was published in 1814 as The Excursion and consisted of nine long philosophical monologues spoken by pastoral characters.

Wordsworth and Dorothy spent the winter of 1798–99 in Germany, where, in Goslar, in Saxony, he experienced the most intense isolation he had ever known. But the result was some of his most moving poetry, including the "Lucy" and "Matthew" elegies and early drafts toward The Prelude.

Upon his return to England, Wordsworth incorporated several of these into the second edition of Lyrical Ballads. Together with the astounding work of his second verse collection, Poems, in Two Volumes (1807), it is often said that the period from 1797-1808 was Wordsworth's great decade.

In 1802, during the Peace of Amiens, Wordsworth returned to France, and in Calais he met his daughter, Anne Caroline, and made his peace with her mother, Annette.

That done he journeyed once more back to England and to marriage with Mary Hutchinson, a childhood friend, and to start another family of three sons and two daughters, although only two children would survive.

In 1805 the drowning of Wordsworth's favorite brother, John, the captain of a sailing vessel, gave Wordsworth the strongest shock he had ever experienced. "A deep distress hath humanized my Soul,"

In 1813, he received an appointment as Distributor of Stamps for Westmorland which had an annual income of £400 gave him the financial security to devote his spare time to poetry and to move his family into Rydal Mount, Grasmere; a beautiful location, which inspired his later poetry.

By the 1820s, the critical acclaim for Wordsworth was growing, though his poetry was losing its earlier vigor and emotional luster. For many years Wordsworth had been assailed by vicious, tireless attacks by the critics. Only with the publication of The River Duddon in 1820, did the tide begin to turn.

Many of Wordsworth's last years were given over to tinkering and revising his poems rather than embark on new works.

His masterpiece, The Prelude, had four distinct manuscript versions (1798–99, 1805–06, 1818–20, and 1832–39) and was published only after the poet's death in 1850.

In 1839 he received an honorary degree from Oxford University and received a civil pension of £300 a year from the government.

With the death in 1843 of his friend and Poet Laureate Robert Southey, Wordsworth was offered the position. He accepted despite saying he wouldn't write any poetry as Poet Laureate. Indeed it is still unfortunate that Wordsworth is still the only Poet Laureate never to write any poems during his time as Poet Laureate.

Wordsworth died of pleurisy on 23 April 1850. He was buried in St Oswald's church Grasmere.

As a poet his work is still avidly read today. He is acknowledged as one of the Romantic Poets, A Lake Poet and a writer of immense talent who gave a voice to many and varied thoughts.

William Wordsworth – A Concise Bibliography

Major Works
Descriptive Sketches (1793)
An Evening Walk (1793)
Lyrical Ballads, with a Few Other Poems (1798)
"Simon Lee"
"We are Seven"
"Lines Written in Early Spring"
"Expostulation and Reply"
"The Tables Turned"
"The Thorn"
"Lines Composed A Few Miles Above Tintern Abbey"
Lyrical Ballads, with Other Poems (1800)
Preface to the Lyrical Ballads
"Strange Fits of Passion Have I Known"
"She Dwelt Among the Untrodden Ways"
"Three Years She Grew"
"A Slumber Did my Spirit Seal"
"I Travelled Among Unknown Men"
"Lucy Gray"
"The Two April Mornings"
"Nutting"
"The Ruined Cottage"

"Michael"
"The Kitten At Play"
Poems, in Two Volumes (1807)
"Resolution and Independence"
"I Wandered Lonely as a Cloud" (aka "Daffodils")
"My Heart Leaps Up"
"Ode: Intimations of Immortality"
"Ode to Duty"
"The Solitary Reaper"
"Elegiac Stanzas"
"Composed Upon Westminster Bridge, September 3, 1802"
"London, 1802"
"The World Is Too Much with Us"
Guide to the Lakes (1810)
"To the Cuckoo"
The Excursion (1814)
Laodamia (1815, 1845)
The Borderers (1842)
The Prelude (1850)

www.ingramcontent.com/pod-product-compliance
Lightning Source LLC
Chambersburg PA
CBHW061253040426
42444CB00010B/2371